UNRAVELLING
7x5 Funda

For Setting-up a Milk Processing Plant

Are you ready to invest in a dairy processing plant?
Before you do, make sure you know the answers to
the 35 questions across 7 sections!

UNRAVELLING
7x5 Funda

For Setting-up a Milk Processing Plant

AMARDEEP SINGH CHADHA

Worldwide Published by
Pendown Press

PENDOWN PRESS

An ISO 9001 & ISO 14001 Certified Co.,

Regd. Office: 2525/193, 1st Floor, Onkar Nagar-A, Tri Nagar, Delhi-110035

Ph.: 09350849407, 09312235086

E-mail: info@pendownpress.com

Branch Office: 1A/2A, 20, Hari Sadan, Ansari Road, Daryaganj, New Delhi-110002

Ph.: 011-45794768

Website: PendownPress.com

First Edition: 2023

ISBN: 978-93-5554-501-5

I lovingly dedicate this book to my Grandmother, the Late Sardarni Veerawali Chadha, whose love and affection were my first introduction to the beauty and goodness of this world. Her unconditional love continues to remain my guiding light even today.

Contents

Who Should Read This Book?

This book is specially intended for aspiring dairy entrepreneurs who are aiming to set up a milk processing plant and also for those who are already in the dairy business and want to expand their existing business by setting up a dairy processing unit.

This book will help them to understand all things they should enquire about before they venture into the milk processing business. To make things easier to understand, it has been divided into 7 Sections, and in every section, we have emphasised 5 critical questions so that a new investor should answer so that they can create a successful milk processing plant.

Therefore anyone interested in making a career in the milk processing business should definitely read this book.

How to Use This Book?

"If I had an hour to solve a problem and my life depended on it, I would use the first 55 minutes to determine the proper question to ask, for once I know the proper question, I could solve the problem in less than five minutes."
~Einstein

This book is a small effort from my side in the vast pool of the dairy industry. It will serve as a hand extended in support to all prospective entrepreneurs by helping them to understand how to set up a milk processing plant.

It's an effort to inform and acquaint the readers with all the queries and their answers about setting up a milk processing unit. The book, I hope, will act as a bridge between the thought of setting up a dairy business and the actual fulfilment of the same.

You could find other dairy books which talk about dairy technology, dairy testing and the microbiology of a dairy. However, they are too technical, which could be good for the dairy fraternity to understand but do not guide them on the practical aspects of running a successful dairy business.

This book is the only one of its kind written solely to enlighten aspiring dairy entrepreneurs in the simple language of business and not in technicalities.

This book will prepare you for your entrepreneurial journey by teaching you all you need to know so that you do not struggle and spend your time and energy on useless issues.

I have personally experienced many such issues and have learned so much while dealing with them.

In this series of books, I have made a sincere effort to provide information and solutions from my vast experience, which no one else is willing to share. And I have done it in the simplest possible way so that it uplifts people who want to enter the dairy processing industry.

I am sure after going through this book; you will be able to decide in which direction you should work to start your business and collect the information.

The book is a clear roadmap to setting up a dairy processing unit.

If you can flesh out the answers and are clear on all (7x5) 35 questions, then you are absolutely ready to set up a dairy processing unit.

There will be no room to make any mistakes during the setting up of the milk processing plant. I am confident that you will be able to establish a successful dairy unit using this book.

I have learned that to succeed in this sector, what you need most are the right kinds of guidance, directions and encouragement from successful entrepreneurs who have **"been there and done that!"**.

There is a definite need for guidance from successful entrepreneurs who have learnt from their mistakes so that new entrepreneurs need not repeat the same.

Take the classic example of the wheel. The wheel is already invented, and the new entrepreneurs just have to use the available knowledge and do not need to experiment all over again.

Similarly, there is a definite need to make a blueprint for establishing and operating a successful dairy business which new entrepreneurs can use and thereby avoid all the mistakes made by their peers and be prepared to face the business challenges.

And this is exactly what I will be sharing with you, candidly and sincerely, in this publication - 7x5 fundamentals of a successful milk processing unit. Others maintain secrecy because of the fear of creating competition. In my opinion, such knowledge is crucial for setting up a successful dairy business and must be shared to create healthy competition and uplift the industry and economy as a whole.

Further, for those readers who have not done so yet, I strongly recommend reading the previous book in this series, **"Establish a Super Successful Mini Dairy Processing Business"**, which will give you deep insights into the dairy business.

About the Author

Hello, my name is **Amardeep Singh Chadha, and I am a specialist in Dairy Equipment Engineering.** Because of my intensive knowledge, deep understanding and extensive experience with the milk processing needs of the small-scale sector, **people acknowledge me as an Expert in Dairy Entrepreneurship.** I have a great passion for sharing my knowledge.

I am the Director at Chadha Sales Pvt. Ltd. (Dairy Equipment Engineers). Academically, I hold a Bachelor's degree in Commerce (B.Com) from Delhi University, a Post Graduate Diploma in Business Management from IILM Delhi, a Master's degree in Business Administration (MBA) from the European University, Belgium and a Diploma in Advance Computer Programming, from ICS Delhi.

I have enhanced my skills as a Certified Milking Machine Specialist from Denmark and have completed a Short-term Dairy course from KVK, NDRI, Karnal. I am also a Certified Manager by the German Federal Ministry of Economic Affairs & Energy.

In addition, I am an elected member of the "Central Executive Committee" of the Indian Dairy Association (IDA) 2022-2025. IDA works on the objective of advancement of dairy science and industry, farming, animal husbandry, animal sciences and its branches, including dairy farming & research on breeding and management of dairy livestock.

The family business of designing, manufacturing and marketing Dairy Equipment was set up by my grandfather, father and my uncle six decades ago, with a very humble beginning.

So, let's begin at the beginning- when I completed my studies abroad and joined my family business. It was a great life; selling dairy machines and instruments and making money was great fun. I spent many comfortable and prosperous years within the confines of my company. I never had the opportunity to venture outside to see my customers and explore the dairy industry in general.

In 2008 we started delivering turnkey dairies to entrepreneurs who wanted to start a dairy business. Thereafter my interaction with dairy enterprises increased a little. Although I was manufacturing machinery side by side, I was witnessing and learning from the entrepreneurship journeys of many dairy entrepreneurs, and I witnessed both successes and failures.

Whenever I heard about a dairy failure, it was heartbreaking for me, and I always felt very frustrated and upset. And one question that kept bothering me was this:

"Why do dairy enterprises fail?"

India is a country of milk lovers, and milk is in abundance. There is a huge consumer base in India, and the dairy business is fairly profitable, but still, some succeed and some fail in this business.

And sadly, I would find no answer to that.

I am sure you must have also often heard that this or that known dairy had closed down as they failed to sustain their business. Each dairy business failure I would learn about anywhere across India, the more I would get inquisitive about the reasons behind their failure.

As per my calculation, dairy businesses should not fail at all as it has the potential for a great ROI and understanding Dairy is a science which can be methodically understood and applied.

There are so many dairy science experts available to learn from. But still, there are failures. This query remained embedded somewhere in the back of my mind for many years. But I was fully occupied with my business, so I was unable to spare any time to analyse it and work on it.

In 2020 Covid came in uninvited, and everyone's life was suspended. As I am a workaholic, I became really worried as to what I would do if I had to stay closed at one place for an indefinite time period.

Then came the day when the whole world shut down due to the pandemic. My office and factories had to come to a stop along with the rest of the world.

It was the momentous first day of the lockdown. Suddenly in the morning, I was struck by an idea!

I thought, why don't I spend my time constructively working on, researching and resolving my long pending pain related to the mysteries of dairy failure?

Finally, through a strange set of circumstances, the Universe gifted me my purpose. I decided that I would put all my energy into this task and take advantage of this time to resolve this gruesome query and find a way to help dairy enterprises in these challenging pandemic-ridden times. I started my endeavour from that very day. When there is a thirst and a sacred intent in your soul to seek something, the Universe provides a path.

I had many case studies already in my records, and as I began studying them in-depth, slowly and steadily, I was able to put my finger on the reason for the foundational mistakes for dairy failures.

And to my surprise, the reasons behind these failures were not complicated. They were occurring due to basic, fundamental reasons, mostly because many secrets were not being revealed by experienced dairy entrepreneurs to the new entrants.

I found that aspiring dairy entrepreneurs were making similar mistakes that others had made when they started their enterprises.

There was no organised knowledge or mentorship that new entrants could draw upon to facilitate their journey and avoid the most common pitfalls. (They sought guidance from other unprofessional dairies, fabricators and other people who, because of their personal interest, hidden motives and unbaked knowledge, caused them enormous losses)

Hence the journey of writing this series of books began so that I could bring out this information to all the aspiring and struggling dairy entrepreneurs to enable them to succeed in their projects with zero failures.

With this intent to serve the dairy industry, I am bringing out a series of books and sharing all the information that I have gathered over my years of experience and expertise for establishing a successful and profitable dairy.

I did the required in-depth research and wrote this book to make people aware of the fundamentals of running a dairy enterprise, which otherwise leads to loss of time, money, energy and sometimes even the project's failure.

I promise that this book will empower dairy entrepreneurs with knowledge and insight that will save them from any future losses.

Milk is widely consumed; it's a complete food and has a special position in the hearts of Indians. I am on a mission to help milk processing enterprises to serve the entire society by providing quality and healthy milk.

By doing this, I believe I am contributing in some way to my bigger goal of creating a healthy world around us.

Today we have achieved new heights, growing multi-folds during the last two decades under my leadership, working along with my brothers. This growth and success, however, has not been a straight-line graph.

The growth has been marked with its own ups and downs, overcoming the numerous challenges & uncertainties that any and every entrepreneur faces.

I am also a founder of the Dairy Explorer Program, which is a framework to provide in-depth understanding and learning on key skills needed for running a successful milk processing business. **It is the platform on which I personally handhold the dairy entrepreneurs and be with them until they succeed in their ventures.**

The reason for creating the Dairy Explorer platform was that many enthusiastic entrepreneurs want to invest in the Dairy sector but have limited knowledge. The lack of knowledge either results in the failure of the venture or the struggle to grow. The Dairy Explorer program provides in-depth knowledge about the various aspects of setting up successful Milk processing units.

Positive feedback in huge numbers proves that aspiring entrepreneurs found it extremely helpful in making decisions regarding entering the Dairy Business after learning through our program.

The Explorer program is designed in a manner that, after attending it, even a layman/first timer is able to take a call, whether the setting up of a dairy falls under their ambit and whether they should go ahead with it or not. And also provides further deeper learning to existing dairy enterprises. It is a very comprehensive and to-the-point program.

It is a kind of reality check that needs to be done when one is ready to take a plunge. There are now around 337 plus Dairy Explorer Graduates who have taken this program and are thriving on their journey towards their dream dairy venture.

Today, I have reached a level of knowledge and experience through which I can lend my hand as an expert in setting up a dairy processing plant. I have worked with more than 250 plus dairy entrepreneurs during the last two decades. I love to work with this close group of entrepreneurs with passion and help them increase their income from the Dairy Business.

I am on a mission to serve this sector by creating 10000 Successful entrepreneurs in the dairy Sector.

You could be the next...

Wishing you overflowing success and profitability.

Yours sincerely

~Amardeep Singh Chadha

*Even if a Bunch of Entrepreneurs get
Motivated and Create Successful Careers in
the Dairy Industry, My Work is Done...*

Acknowledgements

I am deeply grateful to the individuals and groups who have supported me throughout the creation of this book. The world is a better place because of those who develop and support others. I am particularly grateful to those who share their time, knowledge, and experience to mentor future leaders.

Nobody has been more important to me in the pursuit of this project than my parents, Sdn. Surjeet Kaur and S. MPS Chadha, whose love and guidance are with me in whatever I pursue. I am eternally grateful for their unwavering support, care, and encouragement. They are truly my ultimate role models.

I also want to express my deepest gratitude to my wife, Kavleen, for her unwavering support and dedication throughout this process. Her love and support have been invaluable, and she has been as essential to the completion of this book as I have.

My children, Anika and Praneet, have also been a constant source of inspiration and joy. Their selfless love and affection have been the driving force behind my desire to create a better future for all of us.

Writing a book is harder than I thought and more rewarding than I could have ever imagined. None of this would have been possible without the support of my brothers, dear Manjeet and dear Jagdeep. Their brotherhood has been a constant source of strength and inspiration for me.

I am eternally grateful to my uncle, S. Baldev Singh Chadha, for his guidance, discipline, love, and respect. He has been a father figure to me, and his support has been instrumental in my success.

I am also thankful to my team at Chadha Sales Private Limited, who have provided me with the opportunities and support to lead a great group of individuals.

Thank you, Mr J.M Saluja, whose support and guidance have crafted the path of writing this series of books. Thank you, Ms Rubi Kumari, for being supportive of my ventures and Thank you, Ms Ritu Gupta, for managing my schedule, which has given me time to express myself.

Foremost, how can I miss thanking all my clients whom I have served over the last so many years and who shared with me the ground realities of business and became the very base that encouraged me to write this book.

A very special word of gratitude to Arsh, Palav, Jenit & Banni; you are a joy to my heart and a delight to my eyes.

Last but not least: I can not express enough thanks to all my nearer & dearer ones who have been with me over the course of the years and whose names are not mentioned in this book because the list lying in my heart is endlessly long and needs a separate book in fact. I apologise for this to the core. In one or the other way, you all are actually the inspiring and guiding force behind all my endeavours.

Above all, I want to thank the Universe for providing me with the opportunity to write and share my knowledge and experience with all of you. I am deeply grateful for the environment that has allowed me to stay focused and bring this book to completion.

~Amardeep Singh Chadha

Chapter 1

What we Learn vs Ought to Learn

The Idea Stage of Starting a Dairy Business

When anyone plans to start a journey of entrepreneurship, they think of multiple options. One of the lucrative options in the food industry is to get into the dairy business. And when they decide to set up a Dairy Enterprise, they begin hunting on the Internet for Dairy Companies, Manufacturers of Dairy Machines, Suppliers of Dairy Processing Units, and so on.

Then, they start contacting them, asking them for quotations and visiting the existing running Dairy Processing Units to find several lucrative options with different permutations and combinations. They start procuring the dairy machines and equipment in faith. It seems to them a sure-shot formula to becoming a successful dairy entrepreneur.

Hence the knowledge comes to them from a number of sources, and mostly it is half-cooked. Usually, the sources will be:

- Marketplace, neighbourhood milk distributors or milk dealers.

- Friends and peers who are already in the business

- Dairy consultants - who may or may not have dairy entrepreneurship experience

- Milk plant sellers - there are plenty of them, and you will find uneducated fabricators without the right knowledge about milk & technology

Is the knowledge gained by them worth it?

Is it enough for them to make a decision?

Are they missing anything?

Is it only about getting milk and processing it?

No, it's not that simple, of course!

So, what they must know but have not been told is this:

To start any business, 'Proper Planning and Knowledge' is the most important key. My years of experience say that one can select the right kind of machinery only when they know the complete picture of their enterprise, such as what products they have to manufacture, what are the needs of their clients and so on.

I am sure you must have heard the parable of blind men and an elephant. It is a story of a group of blind men who have never come across an elephant before and who learn and imagine what the elephant is like by touching it.

Each blind man feels a different part of the elephant's body, but only one part, such as the Leg, Trunk or Tusk. They then describe the elephant based on their limited experience, and their descriptions of the elephant are different from each other. Like one describes the Elephant's Leg as a Pillar, the other says by touching its Trunk that it's a Python and the Tusk as a Sword.

The moral of the parable is that humans tend to claim absolute truth based on their limited, subjective experience as they ignore other limited, subjective truths. Because of this tendency, most of the time, you do not get a clear picture of the actual requirements for setting up a perfect wholesome Dairy Processing Unit.

Generally, when someone thinks of setting up a Milk Processing Unit they focus on the milk processing part without understanding the fact that milk processing is just one section of the Dairy Enterprise. He starts **operating from what is available instead of what is required and gets into a trap.**

Budding entrepreneurs get loads of advice and suggestions from as many people as they meet and discuss their plans. All these suggestions and advice are based on their self-experiences and backgrounds. Everyone is in haste to give solutions and suggestions without understanding the out-and-out condition of someone's distinctive requirements.

When they research, they find companies who are selling dairy machinery and they try to learn from them, and they can provide what they are experts in. They read books on dairy which talk about dairy technology, but no one talks about what a starter should know and what is required for them to know.

Here I would like to share one statement on the dairy business which is very important and makes it easier to understand the dairy business. The statement is **"Dairy Business ends up being very dynamic and situational"**.

This means there is no single fixed template for each & every situation when setting up a successful dairy business. The knowledge comes through years of working in different situations and different regions. And I have shared my experience in the chapters to follow.

Each dairy entrepreneur may have different sets of operations, product mix, marketing ways, target Customers, consumer preferences, available resources, raw material availability, capital requirement, working capital requirement etc.

Each individual has to work out the best option, which could work out in their location and circumstances.

When you get the answers to the 35 criticals in the following pages, your efforts and research are required so that it shall become easier for you to arrive at the best option.

This book will enlighten new entrepreneurs looking to enter the dairy business with **"what they should know, what they should research, and what clarity and information they should have"** before they invest in a dairy processing plant.

There are two phases when one starts working on any business, specifically setting up a dairy processing plant:

- Planning Phase
- Executing Phase

Why is the Planning Phase so Important???

Planning may not be the most enjoyable component of managing projects, but it is the most vital part of reducing risk and failure rates. Planning is needed to identify desired goals, reduce risks, avoid missed deadlines and ultimately deliver the agreed product or service. Without careful planning business is almost certainly guaranteed to suffer.

What is the Importance of the Execution Phase ???

The execution phase turns your plan into action. It helps to keep work on the track, organise the unit, manage timelines and make sure the work is done according to the original plan. The execution phase is usually the longest phase in the life cycle of a business and consumes the most energy and resources. It is pretty evident by now how crucial it is to ensure your plans are realised with clinical precision and minimal deviation.

What is more Important: Planning or Execution?

You can understand the importance of execution through this quote;

> *"The perfect plan, poorly executed will fail.*
> *A lousy plan, well executed, is often successful".*

Execution is one of the most important aspects of business planning. Without effective execution, a business plan will not be successful.

But that does not mean that planning is not important at all. Planning helps us foresee those things that can help us identify and achieve our goals and tip off the execution method. Planning helps us to be accountable for what we do. People who jump to the execution phase without proper planning make mistakes and fail.

A quote on planning can help you understand this better,

"Plans are of little importance, but planning is essential."
~Winston Churchill, former British Prime Minister.

When we talk about giving our time for any business we get into, we need to give considerable time for planning. A lot of new entrepreneurs jump into the execution phase too quickly. To choose the correct path, we should give 80% of our time to planning and 20% time to execution. A well-planned project will always take less time to execute. So planning is the key component where we need to spend our time before putting any single rupee into execution.

Chapter 2

Asking the Right Questions??? What you Must Know.

Before going further, I want to quote a statement by Edward Hodnett that says,

> *"If you don't ask the right question, you don't get the right answer. A question asked in the right way often points to its answer. Asking questions is the ABC of diagnosis. Only the inquiring mind can solve the problem."*

No one can make you an expert. No one can deliver the whole knowledge which comes with experience and working for so many years in an industry or a specific field. But, I can guide you and help you acquire the insight that can help you to recognise the questions you should ask regarding your business.

When you are in the planning phase to set up a Dairy Processing Unit, This would be the most important information:

What to research? Which areas should you be aware of etc.? You must know the right questions which can help you to start perfectly and grow. If you know the right questions, only then can you have the right answers,

I point again. If you don't have the questions, likewise if you don't have the right questions, you cannot start the right planning for your dairy business. As we now know, **"Dairy Business ends up being very Dynamic and Situational"**, so there will not be one answer to the same questions.

How would you get the Right Answers???

What question to ask can be a bit of a challenging task, one might think. But actually, it is really simple. To zero down on the most relevant queries, all you need is a head full of questions.

Let's consider an example to understand this.

Most of you surely would have felt this at some point in time. Suppose you are en route and experience hunger; you automatically start seeing food outlets. As our mind begins to identify more shops selling food items, we hear people talking about recipes. We access social media, and we see a cookery video appear. The delicious aroma of our favourite food just starts appearing from nowhere. Have you ever thought about how and why this happens?

This happens because, at that particular time, your brain and your thought process revolve around your hunger. **And essentially, this is but a response to the query that our mind is trying to find a solution to.**

Let's take an example of where we pose a question to our mind. We ask ourselves, where can we buy milk from? As a response to the query, our mind will start identifying places and resources which we can buy milk from. For that, if you are constantly thinking about the question, "From where to get milk?" **Answers to this question will start pouring in front of you with hundreds of options and mediums to choose from.**

As I mentioned at the start, you need to get the answers to 7 x 5 = 35 questions and get clear answers before making up your mind to set up a dairy processing unit.

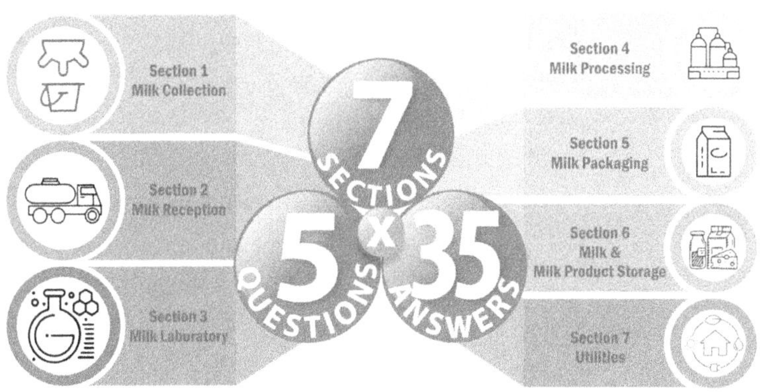

What are these 35 Questions?

I have already shared with you that there are

7- sections of the dairy business.

Each of these 7 sections has some critical parameters, but we are focusing on the 5 – criticals important for the success or failure of the Dairy Business.

And hence, we say seven x (multiplied by) five, thirty-five questions.

Master them, and you are on the right path.

So, what are these seven sections which one must know?

Chapter 3

The Seven Sections of a Milk Processing Plant

For planning a dairy processing unit, we need to plan every aspect of it. When we think of setting up a dairy processing business, normally, we focus primarily on the plant and machinery required for setting up the dairy project.

In this chapter, you will be acquainted with different sections of the dairy. These sections of the dairy processing plant have been segregated solely to understand the importance of each section.

Hereafter we will dive deeply into each section, and this understanding of each section will help plan your dairy processing unit minutely, leaving no surprises in the execution of the same.

The purpose of splitting the dairy processing unit into these seven sections is to give you clarity about the business in totality.

Just like a human body, all the organs must work in synchronisation; these seven sections must work as a single unit to be a healthy & successful unit.

If the legs refuse to walk or the heart refuses to pump, or the lungs refuse to breathe, the body will become sick and die. All the organs have to be healthy for a healthy body. In the same way, all seven sections of milk processing units must be taken care of and work perfectly, and only then can it be a healthy business.

What are these Seven Sections?

1. **Milk Collection Section:** For any dairy to start, we should first arrange for the main raw material, which is milk. A proper model for milk collection is needed to sustain the processing. Milk collection is in itself a complete business model as many people are in the business of just milk collection. If we design our milk collection business model well, we will create a strong foundation for our dairy enterprise.

2. **Milk Reception Section:** It's about receiving the milk at your unit, where you will accept it for further processing. Before milk reaches your processing unit, there are logistics involved with transporting the milk from the collection point to the place of processing and receiving it safely. A healthy reception system shall go a long way to manufacture good quality products and comply with the standards of milk and milk products sold in the market.

3. **Laboratory Section:** At the time of receiving the milk, it should go through detailed testing in a well-equipped laboratory to meet all quality compliances. The third

section of the plant is the Milk Laboratory. Depending upon the scale of operation, it could be a simple laboratory to test fat and SNF and check for adulteration or an elaborate one with analytical testing, bacteriological testing, packing material testing, other raw materials/ inputs testing, products testing and so on.

4. **Milk Processing Unit Section:** Milk Processing is not merely pasteurisation/thermal treatment of the milk. There are different aspects in processing depending upon the products - fermented products or coagulated products, or fat-based products to be manufactured. It also concerns Process, Monitoring, Standards and Quality.

5. **Packing Section:** Different products need different types of protection and hence different packing materials. The type of packing and size of packing shall also depend on retail or bulk selling. Packing is a coordinated system of preparing goods for transport, distribution, storage, retailing and use of the goods. Packing is often referred to as the - Silent Salesman. These decisions have to be made on various inputs, which are explained in detail in the respective chapter that follows.

6. **Storage Section:** The type of storage facility is decided based on the purpose, duration, and environment and considering the perishable nature of milk and milk products.

7. **Utility Section:** Milk processing needs two main processes, or rather three - heating, cooling and mechanisation, and hence needs hot water or steam, iced water and electricity. A number of options are available for each type of utility, and the business has to take a call on them depending on its optimum needs. In addition, a large quantity of water is needed. Generally, 2-3 times the milk handled, for cleaning the equipment, tanks, pipelines, etc. Compressed air may be required if one goes for automation. The right selection of utilities is important, or else it may adversely affect the processing cost and, thus, the profitability of the unit.

Now that you know about the components of a dairy business, in the following chapters, we shall focus on our primary objective:-

**35 questions - 7 sections x 5 critical questions
in each section**

Chapter 4

Milk Collection: Section 1

Milk collection is a crucial step in having a successful milk processing business, as it is the process of gathering raw milk from farmers or other sources and bringing it to the processing facility. The efficiency and effectiveness of the milk collection process can have a significant impact on the overall success of the milk processing business. A steady and reliable supply of raw milk of good quality is essential for maintaining consistent production and meeting customer demand and industry standards.

While planning to make a fail-proof system for milk collection, the 5 critical questions for which you need to seek the answers are as under:

Q1: What Type of Milk is to be Collected?

It is very important to be very clear about what kind of surplus milk shall be available for collection in your location, and accordingly, the end products have to be commensurate with it.

- Would it be cow's milk?

- Would it be buffalo's milk?

- Would it be mixed milk?

- And from how far will we be collecting the milk?

As I mentioned earlier, the dairy business is very dynamic and situational. Each area would have a distinct type or proportionate milk availability. Some places could be cow milk belts; some could be buffalo belts. Or it could be mixed cow and buffalo milk or even goat milk. So the first answer you need to seek is the type of surplus milk available to you for collection. The planning of your Dairy Enterprise would start with that, having decided on the location of the project.

Alternatively, you should do a survey of the region and select the location where you could collect the milk as needed for your end products. It is important to know that transportation cost is one major factor which can make or break a Dairy. Hence there has to be a synchronisation between the type of surplus milk available, end products, distance & transportation costs and the location.

Answers to these shall help you take a major decision about the location as well.

Q 2: What is the Price of Milk in your Area?

It is the deciding factor and impacts your margins and the selling price. But before the price, one must understand the prevalent payment methods for milk. It may be quantity (litres or Kgs) based or quality based, either analytical quality -(fat basis, SNF basis, two-axis basis or total solids basis) or bacteriological quality (as determined by MBR time) and in addition subject to bonus/ penalty based on absence/presence of adulterants, preservatives, neutralisers, etc.

One should try to find the answers to the questions related to the milk price-

- What would be the price of the milk you plan to buy at your place?

- How are you going to calculate it?

- How are you going to record the price of milk?

- How is the price of milk being influenced in your area?

- Do you buy milk in litres?

- Do you buy milk in kg?

- Do you buy milk with fat?

- Do you buy milk by testing Fat and CLR?

- Do you buy milk by testing Fat and SNF?

- What are the factors affecting the price of milk in your area?

Fixing the purchase price of the milk is a crucial task. There is no single method to calculate the price of milk.

So, you have to work with your producers and farmers on the method of pricing, which shall ensure that you get the quality and quantity of milk as required and do not get trapped and pay higher than an optimum price.

Milk prices in different regions also depend upon the demand for milk and the availability of milk in the area. Some regions have higher and some states have lower production of milk hence the price differences. So the milk price varies from region to region. Seasonal variations in milk production and hence availability is also a governing factor for the price of milk. The lean and flush season production ratio may be as high as 1:3.

In certain states, there are government subsidies and policies which also affect the pricing of milk. We also need to understand the selling behaviours of the milk producers and act accordingly. In some places, cow milk and buffalo milk have different pricing, and some pay the same amount.

The determination of the price of milk in an informal/ unorganised market is purely a qualitative process and depends partly on the local demand and partly on the presence of organised buyers in the region.

On the contrary, in the organised sector, milk price is determined based on some specified quantitative parameters. These parameters usually constitute the percentage of Fat, Solid-not-Fat and Protein in milk. In India, the double-axis or dual-axis system of milk pricing is commonly followed in the organised milk market.

The dual axis pricing policy based on fat contents and SNF for fixation of procurement prices of milk has been considered scientifically rational. The price is mainly determined by the percentage of the fat content of the milk. Incentives for better quality milk and penalties for not meeting minimum acceptable standards are prevalent in the organised dairy sector in India.

Q3: Source of Milk Collection - Who will be Your Suppliers?

From whom are you going to buy it? The collection of milk in a dairy is the primary task. The entrepreneur should be very clear about the collection of milk, whether the collection is directly being procured from the local farms or the procurement has to be done from an organised milk collection centre or a combination of both. This means that one should be very clear about the source of milk procurement.

- Are you going to procure milk from Dairy Farms?

- Will you be procuring milk from contractors?

- Would you be buying milk by appointing or liaisoning with milk agents in the villages?

- Or will you be collecting milk directly from a milk producer or homegrown farmer?

- Would you be picking up milk yourself?

- Or will the milk be delivered to your processing unit?

This aspect must be very clear before you design your milk processing section.

Q4: What would be the Number of Collections and their Ratio?

This has an effect on the collection costs. Hence you must definitely ask this question:

- What would be the number of collections a day?

- Are you going to collect it in the morning only?

- Or are you going to collect morning and evening at both times?

- What would be the ratio of the morning and evening milk collected?

Milking of cattle is done twice: morning and evening. So ideally, there should be a collection of milk in the morning and the evening as well.

But it is not that way all across the country.

It depends on the culture of the place, tropical nature and the development of the region. It is seen that in places where there is low development or in hilly areas, or where roads are not developed, milk is collected only in the mornings, and farmers generally are not able to supply it in the evening.

The ratio of milk collection in the morning and the evening could be different in different places where morning and evening collections are done. You need to find out what ratio milk collection is done in your area, whether you collect milk in the morning only or at both times; morning and evening. If you collect the milk both times, what is the ratio of milk collection in the morning and the evening? Is it 50:50 or 60:40, or 70:30, You have to understand this while planning up the milk collection.

Q5: What is Your Collection Procedure?

There can be many different ways of collection, such as:

1. Directly go to the producer's place, test the milk, collect milk in your container and bring it to your unit.

2. Set up a milk collection centre and let producers come there with the milk and then bring it to the unit as raw unchilled milk.

3. Set up a milk collection-cum-chilling centre, collect the milk, chill it at 4 deg C and then bring it to the unit as raw chilled milk.

4. Third-party collection- outsourcing to the contractor.

5. Collecting from the big individual farms.

It is needed to find the best method suited in terms of logistics and quality control of the milk. Ask the following questions

- How will you be collecting milk?

- What would be the right way for you?

- What are the standard practices in your area?

- Where do you want to put up a collection centre?

- Do you procure fresh milk or chilled milk from the chilling centre?

- Would you collect milk after testing the milk? If yes,

then what type of testing is prevalent in your area?

- How do they test?

- Do you cool the milk and then bring it to a Dairy Processing Unit?

- Or are you going to bring fresh milk?

- What are the ways and means to do so?

- Which procedure do farmers trust?

Answers to the above questions are guaranteed to help you in setting up an optimum milk collection method.

Chapter 5

Milk Reception: Section 2

This chapter is about the milk reception system, which means actually receiving the milk collected at the processing unit.

Milk reception is the first point of contact for raw milk and other ingredients that will be used to produce dairy products. The milk reception process plays a critical role in ensuring the quality and safety of the final products.

A good milk reception system will ensure the quality of milk received, prevent its deterioration, enhance the keeping quality and safety of the final products, as well as in meeting the industry standards and sustainable practices and result in the best end products.

What are the 5 critical questions one needs to answer?

Q1: What is the Format of Milk Delivery at the Reception?

The number one question is how the milk would be delivered to your milk processing unit. The milk reception should have a specified area - a milk reception dock to receive the milk through cans, or there should be a facility at the unit to receive the milk through road milk tankers and a facility to transfer the milk to the receiving & storage tank. It depends on the collection system adopted - raw unchilled milk by cans or raw chilled milk by road milk tankers.

Find the answers to these questions:

- Would it be through cans?

- Would it be through tankers?

- Or would it be through both?

Q2: What would be the form of Milk Storage at the Milk Reception?

In the milk reception section, received milk has to be stored and has to be chilled to secure the quality of the milk. For a mini dairy, a Bulk Milk Cooler can be placed for chilling and storage and for bigger units, you can use storage tanks with plate milk chillers to chill and store the raw milk.

Further, if you are dealing with different end products, separate storage is needed for cow milk, buffalo milk, goat milk etc.

- So, how is it going to be stored?
- Are you going to store cow milk separately?
- Are you going to store buffalo milk separately?
- Are you going to store mixed milk altogether?
- Are you going to separate A1 milk and A2 milk?

So you have to make this decision: how are you going to store the milk at the milk reception when it arrives at your dairy processing unit or your shop or at the place of receiving the milk?

Q3: What will be the Quantity of Milk Received at the Reception?

Now when you receive the milk at your milk reception,

- Would it come in small quantities?
- Or would it be in bulk quantities?
- Would it be one time a day?
- Or more than once a day?

The pattern shall decide the traffic visiting and hence the design of the milk reception area in terms of facilities, capacities of equipment and selection of machinery to be provided at the milk reception area to facilitate smooth reception of milk.

Q4: What would be the Temperature of Milk?

The fourth question to understand is the temperature of the milk that will come at your reception.

- Will it be received at the ambient temperature, say 35 degrees?

- Or will you be receiving chilled milk at 4 degrees Celsius?

This would have a significant impact on Milk reception to control the growth of microorganisms, hence bacteriological quality, further processing parameters, as well as in calculating the refrigeration load for the milk Reception section.

Q5: What would be the Norms for Accepting and Rejecting milk?

The fifth question is, how are you going to accept and reject the milk at your milk reception? It is essential that some norms for accepting or rejecting the milk are decided in line with the requirements of the quality of milk to be collected.

It is understood that good quality milk will be passed & accepted, and any adulterated milk or neutralised or added preservatives milk shall be rejected.

Any milk which is borderline may be accepted with some penalty. Complete clarity on the subject is required. It must be understood that there is no universal formula for accepting and rejecting milk, and it has to be situational. Hence need to have a checklist and SOP.

The best is also to find out the general practices of accepting and rejecting the milk around your place of work as there would be a competition in milk collection as well, and you would require the milk to run your unit all the time. Different locations have their own practices of accepting and rejecting milk which you should know by doing research in your planning phase itself.

It also depends on what you want to sell to the market and the suitability of raw milk for your processes to get the desired product you want to make.

If you want to accept cow milk/buffalo milk/both, fresh /chilled milk, what should be the Fat & SNF percentage? Say if you are producing curd, then you could have a different norm. If you are just selling Cow milk, you have a different norm. If you are just making khoya or any specific product, then you could have different norms.

For example, if you would like to sell full cream milk in the market of fat 6% and collect low-fat milk, say with 3% fat, then you would not be able to produce the full cream milk, or you may have to add a low fat/skimmed milk based variant which shall increase the processing cost. Another example says you want to prepare curd with high SNF, say 9.5%, and if you get milk at reception with, say, 7.5% SNF, then you need to add costly additional milk powder to make desirable curd.

Hence, there is a need to create accepting or rejecting norms of the milk, or you can also encourage or discourage by keeping bonuses on the desirable milk and penalising the undesirable milk.

Chapter 6

Laboratory: Section 3

The quality of raw milk is the primary factor determining the quality of milk products.

Good-quality milk products can be produced only from good-quality raw milk. Good-quality raw milk has to be free of off-flavours, abnormal colour and odour. Good-quality milk should be low in bacterial count, free of adulteration and should be of standard composition and acidity.

Since producing milk with high quality is not in your hand, you can only test the quality of milk being received at the processing unit. And to test the quality, there is a need to set up a laboratory at the dairy processing unit. The hygienic quality of milk is critical and important to manufacture safe & long-life milk and milk products.

The questions that one must answer before setting up the quality control laboratory are as under

Q1: What would be the Tests and Testing Equipment?

What are the tests you need to perform to ensure the quality of milk? And what are the apparatus and equipment needed to run those tests?

- Which method will you be selecting to check the composition of milk with respect to fat & SNF, the main ingredients of milk?

- How will you have trained manpower to check the organoleptic quality of milk?

- What instruments in the lab would check the basics, which are acidity, density, stability to heat, and suitability to manufacture products?

- How will you check the bacterial load of milk so that you can estimate how much time your milk will get spoiled?

- How will you check the presence of adulterants, neutralisers and chemical preservatives?

- Are you going to test the milk only for fat & SNF/ analytical tests, or shall you also be checking the bacteriological quality? Have you made provision for that?

Affirmative answers will ensure that you will create a good laboratory.

Q2: How will you Authenticate the Tests.

- How will you authenticate that whatever test you will be testing has been done correctly and is quality compliant?

- How are we going to ensure that the testing equipment being used is reliable, certified and calibrated?

- Do your suppliers trust your testing methods and the equipment?

Q3: How will You be keeping Records?

This is important to trace back the source or cause in case of any consumer complaint.

You will have to ensure proper monitoring of quality round the clock on various parameters, which are important not only to prevent the loss of milk but also for the purpose of satisfying your suppliers, your customers as well as the regulatory authorities.

- Proper record-keeping shall help you resolve disputes with suppliers.

- It shall help to win the trust of your customers.

- And, importantly, satisfy the regulatory authorities and ensure that the products being sold are as per the minimum & declared standards.

Q4: What Other Tests will be there Apart from Milk and Milk Products?

When we set up our dairy laboratory, we focus on laboratory wares for milk and milk products and consider setting up our laboratory with those instruments only. But your laboratory should be equipped with other tests also besides tests for milk and milk products.

Milk is the major raw material which is almost 90% of the total input; yet, there are other materials which require testing.

- What facility will we have to test the quality of water used for cleaning, adding to products and drinking? Is it chemically and bacteriologically safe?

- How will we be testing the calorific value of the fuel being used? HSD may be adulterated with kerosene; wood may be wet or solid fuels may be made heavy with soil/dust.

- How will we ensure that the packing material being used has proper bursting strength, proper sealing properties, and proper gauge/gsm?

Failure to check the material may result in inefficiencies and high operating & processing costs.

Q5: Detection of Additives in Milk and Milk Products?

Of late, there has been rampant adulteration of milk, and water is the main adulterant that producers resort to. But besides water which is not so harmful unless the quality of water is bad, there are a number of chemical adulterants and additives which the producer/middlemen may add, greed being the driving force. For example, urea, starch, vegetable fat, glucose, etc.

If the milk turns acidic, it is likely to curdle on boiling, and hence producers/handlers may use neutralisers.

To prevent bacteriological spoilage, chemical preservatives may be added. All these are harmful and illegal.

- Check if the proposed lab has a facility to test the presence of these additives.

- If the planned tests are rapid platform tests, or do they take time?

- What is the reliability of these tests?

- What are the threshold levels which can be detected by these tests, and are these approved by FSSAI?

- What are the common adulterations in your area of business?

Chapter 7

Milk Processing: Section 4

Milk processing facilities can have many permutations & combinations depending on the product mix, milk to be processed per day, manual or semi-automatic or fully automatic, catering to retail or bulk customers, is it B to C or B to B, and so on.

One important thing that must be understood is that there is no single process or equipment to manufacture any product or do any processing. You cannot just put milk in the machine and get out your curd or butter, or icecream. There are a number of steps involved in manufacturing, and they are called unit operations.

Hence the questions about milk processing which one must seek are as under:

Q1: Have you Decided on the Quantity of Milk to be Processed Per Day?

- Will you be working one shift a day or two shifts or24 hours a day?

- Will you do the milk processing only in the morning or both morning and evening?

Answers to this shall help decide the size of the processing line in terms of litres per hour if it is continuous or batch. For example, a milk pasteurisation line can be of, say, 500 litres per hour, and curd manufacturing can be done in a batch of 200 litres. Equipment capacity has an impact on the capital cost of the project. A wrong selection may result in higher capital as well as low utilisation and hence higher processing costs.

Q2: What shall be your Product Mix? What shall be your By-Products, if any?

Since each product needs a different set of equipment, deciding the product mix, products to be manufactured, and the maximum quantity per day has to be decided. Have you taken that decision depending upon your judgement of the locality, your market, customer's preferences, etc.?

There are likely to be certain by-products when you decide on the main products.

For example, if you are procuring high-fat milk (say buffalo milk), and your clients need low-fat milk, say Toned milk, you will be left with some surplus fat as cream during standardisation. Will you sell cream as such or convert it to butter or ghee as by-products?

In the process of manufacturing Paneer, a lot of Paneer whey goes down the drain. You may like to recover the fat as whey cream, which is a by-product. New technologies and products from whey are being developed as beverages to be manufactured as by-products. You may decide about them, although the capital cost for these technologies is high at present.

Q3: What Type of Milk do you want to Launch?

If you have decided to sell only milk, you have to be clear about the following

- Are you going for raw, unchilled fresh milk without any processing or raw chilled fresh milk?

- Would you be going for pasteurised milk so that the shelf life of milk is prolonged? If pasteurised, will it be homogenised or non-homogenised?

Q4: What are the Variants of the Milk you want to Produce?

Having decided about the milk and the process, the next question which needs an answer is about the variant. FSSAI has prescribed standards for different variants of milk, and you have to take a call on the variant.

Will it be skimmed, double-toned, toned or full cream?

Will it be goat milk, cow milk or buffalo milk?

Caution: If the packed milk does not mention any standard, it is assumed to be Buffalo milk, and the FSSAI inspector shall check the samples as Buffalo milk only.

- Do you want to sell standardised milk?
- Do you want to sell toned milk?
- Do you want to sell skimmed milk,
- or do you want to sell double-toned milk
- or do you want to sell full-cream milk
- or do you want to sell cow milk
- or buffalo milk,
- or do you want to sell low-fat buffalo milk?

Similarly, there are standards for the products, also as low-fat Paneer and standard Paneer, different variants of Khoya - Pindi, Dhap and Danedaar etc.

So, you should have a crystal clear plan of what variants you want to make and how much quantity is to be produced in a day.

Q5: How will You Utilise Surplus or Returned Milk?

There are chances, at least in the initial stages, that the milk sent to market, if remaining unsold, shall come back. Milk sourcing is something which is a long-term association between farmers and processors. One cannot decide on a day-to-day basis whether to receive the milk from the farmer or not unless being sourced through some intermediary/ contractor etc., who shall also require advance intimation.

- So, what do you do with the milk which is returned from the market?

- Or are you left with surplus unprocessed or unutilised milk?

This has to be considered at the planning stage. Or else you will end up going in for a distress sale, selling it to local halwais or to other units at whatever price you can fetch or converting it into products like Khoa or Paneer, which can be cold stored and are less perishable than milk, reducing the bulkiness. This gives a cushion in a short time, and in a long time, milk procurement can be adjusted. Your processing unit should be designed in such a way that in any of the above cases, the milk can be utilised, and you are saved from any losses.

Milk & Milk Products Packing: Section 5

What does the customer see first on receiving your product? It is the packaging of the product. The packing of a product influences the first impression a customer has about the quality of the product. Nicely packed products attract the customer and are picked from the shelf or delivered to homes faster.

Proper packaging can help to protect and preserve the quality and safety of dairy products while also making them appealing and convenient for consumers to purchase and use. Overall, packaging decisions in dairy processing can greatly impact the product's appeal, safety, and sustainability. Therefore it is important to make well-informed decisions to ensure the success of the product.

There are other aspects to packing also, which need to be answered.

Q1: Before going Further, You need to ask Yourself how You Wish to Reach Your Customers.

- Are you offering them packed milk or loose milk?

- Will you go to customers (door delivery) or

- Will the customers come to you?

This shall be helpful in deciding whether to install fixed vending machines or mobile vending machines or pack the milk in single-use packets or reuseable packets.

And if you are going for bulk sale, the requirement shall completely change. You may have to deliver milk in bulk cans to institutions, say, schools, hospitals, and caterers or in a transport tanker to the bulk customers. So you need to decide:

- Do you want to sell it as loose milk?

- Or do you want to sell it in bulk only,

- Do you want to sell milk in pouches,

- Or through bottles,

- Or do you want to sell it through milk vending machines?

How you want to sell is a decision you need to make based on what is good for your market. You can have one way or multiple ways again; it depends upon the marketing strategy you make.

Packing also depends on what products you want to make, i.e. if there is curd, there will be Matka packing, Cup packing and Pouch packing also. For Paneer, you can go with vacuum packing or loose packing, depending on the product.

No matter what your choices are, all these decisions have to be defined by you in the planning stage of the project itself.

Q2: What will be the Pack Sizes?

If you are going to pack the milk, will you be going for one size of pack, say 500 ml or different sizes, 200 ml, 500 ml, 1000 ml or even 5000 ml, to cater to the different market segments? This helps you in deciding whether to go for one or multi-milk packing machines and to plan your investments in packing material.

Q3: Will You go in for Premium or Competitive Selling?

This is a very relevant question and depends on the marketing strategy and the audience you wish to cater to. The foremost decision to be taken is:

- Are we selling our milk at a premium?

- Or do we want to sell milk at competitive rates?

With this decision, we can drive towards the selection of what and how our packed product shall appear. The quality of packing material and labelling on the packet is also a vital factor in packing. The packing material should be food-grade.

Easy to pick up and handle. Easy to open and dispense etc., so it all depends upon whether we are going for a premium or competitive pricing strategy.

Q4: How Far Will You Deliver?

We need to define the distance between the processing unit and the place of consumption. (the place where the customers are located)

- Sometimes it may be advantageous that the milk is transported in bulk to the place of consumption, and it is packed and distributed as per needs. So a packing station shall be set up near the customer.

- Or it can be packed and transported to a cold store, and from there, it is distributed to the customers. This is especially feasible in the case of B to C distribution.

- Or it may be perfectly ok to house everything in the same place when the distance is not too long.

These parameters help decide the kinds of distribution vehicles, the location of packing stations, the location of the cold store, the need to have a cold chain etc.

Distance also affects the quality of packing material which can withstand the journey and keep the milk safe.

Q5: What are the Government Guidelines?

Lastly, an awareness and an understanding of the laws related to packed products are essential to success.

- What information needs to be printed on the package? Will it be printed online?

- Or are you going to use pre-printed packing material?

- What are the recycling norms of the state, especially for plastic sachets?

- Are there any environmental guidelines on the packing?

- Is there a chance or regulation of the plastic ban?

- Is your packing as per the guidelines of FSSAI?

- Does your packing follow the Weights and Measures regulations?

Chapter 9

Storage of Milk and Milk Products: Section 6

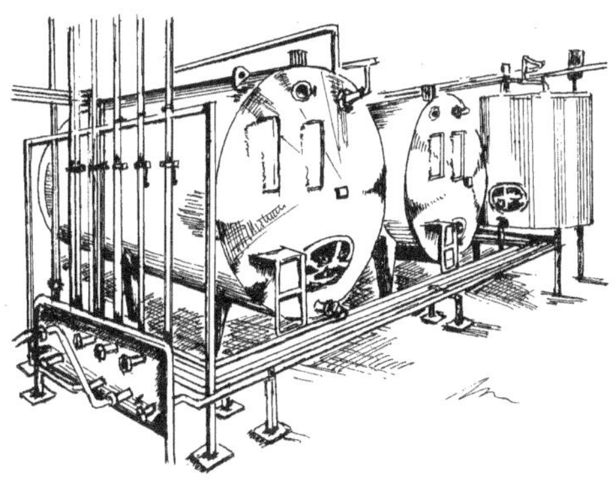

Storage in a dairy processing plant allows the plant to hold and maintain a consistent supply of raw milk and other ingredients, which is necessary for ensuring a steady production of dairy products. Additionally, proper storage conditions are necessary for maintaining the quality and safety of the raw materials and finished products. This includes maintaining the correct temperature and humidity, as well as protecting the materials from contamination. Finally, efficient storage practices can help to optimise the use of space and reduce waste, which can help to improve the overall efficiency and profitability of the dairy processing plant.

Now, here's the sixth section is storage; interestingly, the dairy industry has five types of storage.

Q1: How Will You Store Raw Milk?

- How will the raw milk be received and stored?

- Will it be received in milk cans as raw unchilled and stored and chilled in Bulk Milk Cooling Tanks?

- Or will it be chilled using heat exchangers and stored in insulated tanks?

- Will it be received from the collection centres as raw chilled milk and stored in uninsulated tanks for immediate processing into milk products?

- Or will it be stored in insulated storage tanks to be processed later?

Based on the above, the equipment/storage tanks shall be selected. The capacity of the storage vessel/BMC shall depend upon the frequency of raw milk receipt.

Q2: How Will You Store Processed Milk?

Once the raw milk is pasteurised, depending upon the variants and the quantity to be apportioned to different products, the sizes of different pasteurised and standardised milk tanks shall be decided. So in your case, what would that be?

Q3: How Will the By-Products be Stored?

- What is the quantity of cream available?

- Will you sell it as raw fresh cream? Store in a milk can and keep in a cold store.

- Or if you are going to make ghee by converting it to cooking butter or directly from cream to ghee. Store in cans or a tank depending upon the quantity.

- If it is to be converted to table butter, pasteurise it in a batch and store it in a cooling cum ageing tank hygienically.

- If whey is to be drained, you may recover fat by separation and let it go. But if it is to be used for by-products, it needs to be clarified, separated (recovery of fat), and then chilled or pasteurised and stored in an insulated tank.

Q4: How Will You Store Packaged Milk and Milk Products?

When the milk and milk products are packed and ready for the market, where will you store the same? For that, you need to have separate cold storage.

The size of the cold store shall depend upon the quantity of packed milk to be stored and the type of the pack. In one square metre of space, up to 500 litres of poly-pack milk can be stored, but if packed in bottles, a maximum of 200 litres of milk can be stored. Curd packed in cups, a maximum of 300 litres will be stored per square metre.

Milk, Curd and Paneer are to be stored at 4 deg c, butter at-10 deg C and ice cream at-25 deg C.

Ghee can be stored at about 25 to 35 deg C/at room temperature.

The capacity also depends upon how long you would store the product.

Hence you would require to decide on storage as per your capacities.

Q5: How Will You Store Packing Materials and Other Ingredients?

Packing material is in direct contact with milk and milk products. So, we have to take care of the proper storage of the packing material, such as pouch packing rolls for Milk/Curd/Lassi pouches, plastic Cups/Matka for Curd, preformed pouches for Paneer etc.

If proper care of packing material is not taken, it may get damaged due to temperature or ingress of moisture or by rodents. It will directly affect the quality of packed products. So, Safe storage of packing material is also important.

Other ingredients required for making milk products, like flavour, colour, emulsifier, salt, sugar etc., also need a suitable place for storage.

- Have you earmarked the area for storage of bulk packing material?
- Is the room moisture free?
- Are there enough pallets or racks to keep the material?
- Is the material protected from dust and rodents?

Answer these, and you are sure to have proper storage space for the packing material in your plant.

Chapter 10

Utilities: Section 7

Utilities are essential for the processing of milk, and it includes water supply, steam generation, iced water, electricity, refrigeration, waste treatment etc. The type and sizes of the utilities have to be selected very judiciously as the processing cost shall depend upon the efficient use of these and provides the necessary services and resources for the plant to function efficiently.

Well-designed utilities can reduce downtime, improve product quality and ensure compliance with regulations, making them crucial for the success of the milk processing plant.

So you should investigate the following even before you finalise the location for your processing plant.

Q1: Have You Checked the Source and Reliability of Electric Power?

A milk processing plant requires a continuous 24 x7 power supply for different operations.

- Is the power supply source reliable?

- Is the grid line available 24/7?

- Is it a single phase or 3-phase?

- What is the peak load power requirement?

- Have you planned power back in case of grid failure?

- Will it be DG or solar power, or a combination of both?

- What shall be the fuel for the DG set? Will it be CNG or HSD? What is economically and readily available? Is there a CNG line in your proximity?

Q2: Have You Checked the Source and Reliability of Water?

A dairy plant needs water, 2 to 3 times the quantity of milk processed daily. Water is required for cleaning, reconstitution of milk, adding to products (lassi or chhach), generation of steam, refrigeration (IBT) and drinking purposes

- Have you estimated the quantity of raw water required?

- Is the water potable? Is it free from heavy metals?

- What is the hardness of water?

- How much soft water is required per day?

- How much RO water is required per day?

- What is the source of water? Is it your own boring or municipal water?

- Or are you recycling the water with zero discharge?

Answer these, and you are sure to have an optimised water plant & storage.

Q3: What will be Your Heating Source?

Most of the processing needs heat treatment of milk to different degrees.

- What is the maximum temperature requirement? Ghee manufacturing and sterilisation need high temperatures, and hence steam is best suited.

- Is a hot water generator good for you, or do you need a steam generator for your products?

- Will the non-IBR boiler suffice your need, or do you have to go for an IBR boiler?

- What is the fuel available locally? Which fuel is more economical to use?

- What are the guidelines for the storage of fuel and disposal of waste, if any, from the fuel?

Q4: What will be the Arrangements for Refrigeration?

As has been mentioned umpteen times, milk is perishable and susceptible to spoilage at room temperature. Its cooling and storage under refrigeration are essential to prolong its shelf life.

- Have you calculated your refrigeration needs? The refrigeration equipment should be capable of maintaining the desired temperatures for milk and milk products storage, processing and transportation

- Will it be an instant type or a storage type refrigeration unit? The refrigeration equipment should be energy efficient to minimise operating costs.

- Does it use Freon or Ammonia? Is the Freon gas being used eco-friendly, permitted legally and not likely to be banned in the immediate future?

- Does it use Glycol? Is the Glycol being used of food-grade quality?

- What is the Backup Plan? It is important to have backup plans in case of equipment failure or power outage, to minimise the risk of milk spoilage or other losses.

Q5: What are the Arrangements for ETP?

An effluent treatment plant (ETP) is necessary for a dairy processing plant because it helps to treat and properly dispose of the wastewater generated by the plant. The dairy processing process generates wastewater that may contain a variety of pollutants, such as organic matter, nutrients, and pathogens. Without proper treatment, this wastewater can pollute nearby water sources and harm the environment. An ETP uses a combination of physical, chemical, and biological processes to remove these pollutants and make the wastewater safe for discharge or reuse. Additionally, in India, there are strict regulations for wastewater treatment and discharge, so an ETP is also required to comply with these regulations. When setting up a milk processing plant, there are several important things to consider in terms of effluent disposal in order to ensure proper treatment and compliance with regulations:

- What are the specific pollutants present in the wastewater generated by the milk processing plant? Common treatment processes include physical, chemical, and biological methods.

- How would you calculate the sufficient capacity of ETP to treat the maximum volume of wastewater that the milk processing plant is expected to generate?

- What is the compliance in accordance with regulations for wastewater treatment and discharge? These regulations may vary depending on the location of the milk processing plant. You need to ensure that it is operating properly and that the treated effluent meets the required discharge standards.

- Will you be using treated effluent for irrigation or other purposes, and whether the water is of suitable quality after treatment?

- An emergency plan should be in place in case of any malfunction or breakdown of the treatment process.

CONCLUSION

In the preceding chapters, I have made an effort to comprehensively cover all aspects related to the sections of milk processing. To summarise, we can conclude that establishing and running a milk processing plant requires a common-sense approach, as the highly perishable nature of milk necessitates a vigilant focus on ensuring milk quality at every step of the handling process.

To achieve this, it is crucial to have a thorough understanding of the 35 key questions, 5 each in the 7 Sections. These are essential to creating a solid and successful milk processing unit. By seeking answers to these 35 questions, you will gain a clear understanding of the steps required to build a milk processing unit that is sure to be successful.

Now that you have gained this knowledge, it is time to put your learning into practice and begin the process of building your own milk processing unit on the path to success.

Thank you for reading this book. It proves you are serious about setting up a successful and profitable milk processing plant. So go ahead, and apply your learnings to establish yourself as a trailblazer in your industry, enjoying the fruits of your labour as profits while contributing to a healthy society.

For those of you who genuinely wish to be the trailblazers in this sector or those who want to scale up your dairy business to the next level in minimum time, I invite you to be a part of the Dairy Explorer Program, where I will personally handhold you and mentor you onto the path of amazing success and profitability in minimum time with minimum challenges.

To enrol for the Dairy Explorer Program, go here:

www.chadha.vip/dxp

To Speak to the Program Manager, you can call +91-8588844771

Email us: info@chadhasales.com

For more updates and success tips, stay connected with us at:

https://www.facebook.com/chadhasales

https://www.instagram.com/chadhasales

https://twitter.com/Chadha_Amardeep

https://www.youtube.com/user/chadhasales1/videos

https://www.linkedin.com/in/amardeep-chadha

The Gift

Making the right decisions may be easy for some and may not be so easy for others. So, if you feel you need further support and hand-holding or have questions unanswered, feel free to avail the Free Gift below:

A Free 90-minute webinar on **Ask the Dairy Expert.** This webinar will further strengthen and review your learnings from this book, and in the webinar, you will also have a further special gift for joining our Dairy Explorer Program.

I am more than ready to help aspiring and existing dairy owners and would be honoured to become a part of your growth journey.

To claim your free gift, email me at **bookgift@chadhasales. com** with your Name, Mobile Number, City and a scanned copy of the proof-of-purchase of this book.

In the subject line, please mention: "Ask the Dairy Expert-Free Gift-7x35".

To learn more about dairy machinery,

visit www.chadhasales.com

To know more about Dairy Machinery, Call here: +91 7864006400

Our Story

Like every successful story, ours is built on the twin pillars of utmost passion and strong determination.

Sardar Makhan Singh Chadha ran a small-scale dairy in pre-partition Punjab. When the tribulations of partition hit India, he moved to Delhi from Pakistan.

Then began a journey of starting everything from nothing. With his grit & determination, coupled with his charm and positive attitude, he started delivering milk on a rented bicycle. Soon he progressed to a small dairy at the Tis Hazari Refugee Camp.

Things took a turn for the business when this ingenious entrepreneur single-handedly imported the Gerber Centrifuge, a milk-testing instrument from Switzerland with little technical training and capital.

The Gerber centrifuge proto-type at that time caught the attention of many other dairy owners. And the visionary became a manufacturer of dairy machinery from a mere supplier of dairy products.

Along with his two sons - Mohinder Paul Singh Chadha and Baldev Singh Chadha, he expanded the business with the production of various machinery and equipment like Cream Separators, Milk Testing Appliances, Lockstoppers, Butyrometers, Aluminium Alloy Milk Cans, and Milk Cooling Tanks.

The legacy has been taken forward by three brothers, Manjeet, Amardeep and Jagdeep. Today, as the pioneers of dairy machinery and equipment, Chadha Sales Pvt. Ltd. is one of the most trusted names in the industry. And together with the new generation, we strive to keep innovating to give our customers the best service possible.

Chadha Sales Private Ltd is a pioneer company in the field of Dairy Equipment and Plants. The company has grown from a micro-enterprise to a large company with customers all across the globe.

Chadha Sales Pvt. Ltd is backed by a professional team of skilled and experienced engineers. The company has a well-equipped in-house production unit with state-of-the-art machines.

There are a number of inspection instruments and testing facilities that help in providing our customers with consistent quality at all times. The company's R&D Department anticipates future needs and works upon them, which keeps the company miles ahead of others.

Apart from being a front-runner in the domestic market, the company caters to the vast need of the quality-conscious market of the world. The company's Indian clientele includes the National Dairy Development Board, Govt. & Private Milk Co-operatives, Dairy Federations, Dairy Farms, Public Sector Undertakings, Multinational Companies etc.

Our Factories are located at Distt Sonepat, (Haryana), and our Corporate office is centrally located in the Capital of India. Delhi.

The torch has been kept alive and burning by Amardeep Singh Chadha, fuelled by his passion for helpingdairy enterprises. This has made him **India's #1 Mentor for starting a Dairy Enterprise.**

Amardeep Singh Chadha is a proven name in the DAIRY INDUSTRY with 23 years of extensive experience. He coaches budding entrepreneurs and dairy owners to obtain absolute clarity on setting up a new dairy enterprise or managing existing dairy units.

Having invested so many years in the Industry, Mr Chadha has in-depth practical knowledge in the area of Milk Quality, Milk Collection, Milk Processing, and Milk Marketing and has first-hand experience with the issues faced in the dairy industry. His Strategic interventions help his mentees attain confidence and create a practical path for their dairy business.

Today we proudly declare that we are in the business of improving the quality and profitability of the dairy business, and we are committed to continuing to do so for eternity in new and innovative ways.